MONTANA

in words and pictures

BY DENNIS B. FRADIN

ILLUSTRATIONS BY RICHARD WAHL

MAPS BY LEN W. MEENTS

Consultant:
    Robert R. Archibald, Ph.D.
    Director, Montana Historical Society

 CHILDRENS PRESS, CHICAGO

For my children: Anthony, Diana,
and Michael Fradin

For their help, the author thanks:

Merle Lucas, who is a member of the Sioux tribe and also the State Coordinator of Indian Affairs of Montana

David Girshick, Catalogue Librarian, Montana Historical Soci
Library

Sun Mountain, Glacier National Park

Library of Congress Cataloging in Publication Data

Fradin, Dennis B
  Montana in words and pictures.

  SUMMARY: Discusses the history, geography, industry, and famous citizens of the "Treasure State."
  1. Montana—Juvenile literature. [1. Montana]
I. Wahl, Richard, 1939-   II. Meents, Len W.
III. Title
F731.3.F7   978.6   80-25023
ISBN 0-516-03926-1)

Picture Acknowledgments:

U.S. DEPARTMENT OF THE INTERIOR, NATIONAL PARK SERVICE— page 2; Photos by W.S. Keller pages 9, 35, 37 (top left, bottom right), 38, by Cecil W. Stoughton pages 5, 43; Photo by Fred Mang, Jr. page 15
TRAVEL PROMOTION UNIT, MONTANA DEPARTMENT OF HIGHWAYS—pages 15 (top left & right), 17, 19, 23, 26, 30 (left), 31, 34(2), 37 (bottom left, top right); Photos by G. Wunderwald pages 11 (left & right), 25 (left); Photo by S. Price page 28.
U.S. DEPARTMENT OF INTERIOR, BUREAU OF LAND MANAGEMENT, BILLINGS—pages 18(2), 21(2), 25 (right), 30 (right), 33.
WESTERN HERITAGE CENTER—page 24(2)
WIDE WORLD PHOTOS—page 20
JAMES P. ROWAN—cover, page 15 (bottom right)
MONTANA STOCK GROWERS ASSOCIATION—page 41
GILCREASE INSTITUTE—page 16
U.S. FORESTERY SERVICE, MISSOULA—page 36
COVER: Glacier National Park, Logan Pass & Hidden Lake

Montana

The word *Montana* (mon • TAN • ah) comes from a Spanish word which means *mountain*. The Rocky Mountains are in the western part of the state. Montana is considered one of the Rocky Mountain States.

Montana is nicknamed the *Treasure State*. In the 1860s gold was the treasure that brought thousands to Montana. Today, large amounts of oil, coal, and copper come from its ground. Good soil is another of the state's treasures. It helps make Montana a leading wheat-growing state.

Do you know what state first sent a woman to the United States House of Representatives (rep • ree • ZEN • tah • tivz)? Or where the Indians won the famous Battle of the Little Bighorn? Do you know what state has more than three times as many cattle as people?

If you haven't guessed, you'll soon see that the answer to all these questions is Montana!

Over 75 million years ago dinosaurs (DINE • ah • sorz) lived in Montana. Triceratops (try • SAIR • uh • tops) was there. He was a peaceful plant eater. Tyrannosaurus Rex (tuh • RAN • uh • sore • us RECKS) wasn't peaceful. He ate other dinosaurs! The last dinosaurs died long before the first people appeared on Earth.

Over a million years ago Montana was cold year-round. This was during the Ice Age. Mountains of ice,

Bison is another name for the North American buffalo.

called *glaciers* (GLAY • sherz), covered northern Montana. In places the ice was over half a mile thick.

People first arrived in Montana at least 10,000 years ago. They are called the Early Hunters. They followed herds of bison and other big animals across the land. Spear points and stone tools of the Early Hunters have been found.

In more recent times, many Indian tribes lived in Montana. Some lived on the level plains in the east. Others made their homes in the Rocky Mountains in the west.

The Blackfeet, Crow, Cheyenne (shy • ANN), Sioux (SOO), and Arapaho (ah • RAP • ah • ho) lived on the plains. These Indians hunted buffalo with bows and arrows. The buffalo meat was eaten. The skins were used to make clothes. Buffalo skins were also used to make tents, called *tepees*.

The Kutenai (KOO • tee • nay), Shoshoni (show • SHOW • nee), and Bannock (BAN • uck) were three of the mountain tribes. These Indians hunted deer and bears. They fished. They ate berries and roots also.

The Indians had the land to themselves for hundreds of years. French fur trappers are thought to have entered Montana in the 1740s. But these men didn't want land. They were after beavers and other furry animals.

In 1803 the United States bought a big piece of land from France. Most of Montana was included. Americans wanted to learn more about the land they bought. President Thomas Jefferson sent Meriwether Lewis (MARE • ih • weather LOO • iss) and William Clark to explore this land.

Lewis and Clark set out from near St. Louis (SAYNT
LOO • iss), Missouri (mih • ZOO • ree), in May of 1804.
They headed west towards the Pacific (pah • SIH • fick)
Ocean. Led by a 17-year-old Indian woman named
Sacagawea (sock • ah • ja • WEE • ah), they crossed the
Montana plains. They went west through the mountains.
Lewis and Clark named the Judith River and other
places in Montana.

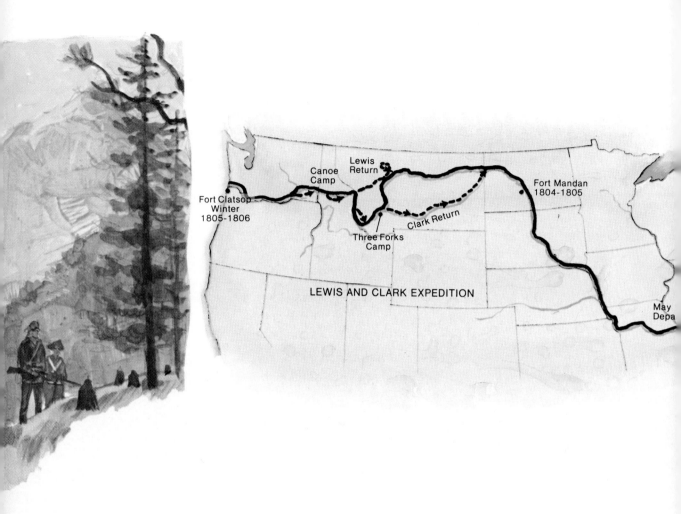

Fort Clatsop
Winter
1805-1806

Canoe
Camp

Lewis
Return

Fort Mandan
1804-1805

Clark Return

Three Forks
Camp

LEWIS AND CLARK EXPEDITION

May
Depa

Lewis and Clark reported that Montana had beavers
and other fur-bearing animals. In the early 1800s, hats
and other clothes were made out of beaver furs. Fur
trappers came to Montana. They caught the animals
themselves. Fur traders came also. They let the Indians
catch the animals. Then they traded blankets and
trinkets to the Indians in exchange for the furs.

Some fur traders were liked by the Indians. A few married Indian women. But as more traders arrived, some Indians felt that one day the newcomers might want land instead of furs. Traders and trappers were sometimes killed by Indians. One man, John Colter (COLE • ter), found himself facing hundreds of angry Indians. The Indians gave Colter a head start and let him run for his life. Colter got away. He lived to discover the area that is now Yellowstone National Park.

Electric Peak, Yellowstone National Park

In 1841, some priests, called *missionaries* (MISH • un • air • eez), came to Montana. They came to teach the Indians about Christianity (kris • chee • AN • ih • tee). Father Pierre Jean De Smet (pea • AIR ZAHN dih SMET) was the leader. He built a church called St. Mary's Mission. Father De Smet planted Montana's first crops— wheat, oats, and potatoes.

In 1846 the American Fur Company built Fort Lewis (later called Fort Benton) on the Missouri River. This fort was the first permanent settlement in what is now Montana. But the fur business was not so important by 1850. Many of the beavers had been killed.

With the fur trade ending, few Americans came to Montana. Other places were easier to get to and had better weather for farming. In fact, some people said that Montana's land was good-for-nothing.

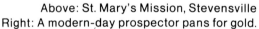
Above: St. Mary's Mission, Stevensville
Right: A modern-day prospector pans for gold.

Then something happened to make people VERY interested in Montana. In 1862 two men found gold at Grasshopper Creek! Thousands headed to Montana to search for gold in the mountains.

Near Grasshopper Creek, a town was built almost overnight. It was named Bannack. Gold was found in other places of southwest Montana. Virginia City and Diamond City were two other gold-mining towns.

One of the most interesting gold finds occurred in 1864. Four men had spent time looking for gold. They hadn't found it. They decided to give themselves one last chance to look. They found gold at a place they named Last Chance Gulch. In time, over twenty million dollars worth of gold was mined from Last Chance Gulch. The town that grew up there was soon named Helena (HEHL • uh • nuh). Today Helena is the capital of Montana.

Only a few people made big gold strikes. Many miners gave up. Some became storekeepers in the mining towns. The storekeepers wound up with gold, too! Miners used gold dust to pay for food and other things at the stores. Saloons and gambling halls were built in the mining towns. The few who struck it rich sometimes lost their gold at the gambling tables.

The mining towns were rough places. There were fistfights and sometimes even gunfights. There were also outlaws who were ready to shoot people down and steal their gold.

A man named Henry Plummer became sheriff of Bannack. It turned out that he was an outlaw, too. He and his gang robbed stagecoaches. You know that a town is rough when even the sheriff's an outlaw!

Men from Bannack and Virginia City formed a *vigilante* (vih • jill • AN • tee) group. Even though they weren't lawmen, they took the law into their own hands. Plummer was hanged. So were many other people thought to be outlaws.

In 1864 Montana became a territory. It wasn't a state yet. It was land owned by the United States. The territorial government made laws to try to bring law and order to Montana.

By 1870 Montana had over 20,000 settlers. The Indians in Montana—and in other areas—grew angry as settlers took their lands. Some Indians fought. Two of the most famous battles between soldiers and Indians occurred in Montana.

The Sioux Indians were angry because their land had been taken in South Dakota. General George Custer was sent to round up the Indians. The Indians were to be pushed onto small pieces of land called *reservations* (rez • er • VAY • shunz). In 1876 the Sioux and the Cheyenne Indians met Custer and his men at the Little Bighorn River. The Indians, led by Crazy Horse, won the Battle of the Little Bighorn. Custer and his men were wiped out in what is sometimes called "Custer's Last Stand." This was one of the few times the Indians won a large fight.

Above left: General George Armstrong Custer
Above: Visitors tour the battlefield at the Little Bighorn.
Left: Soldiers at Fort Union
Below: Gravestones at Custer National Cemetery

Painting of Chief Joseph's surrender in 1877

The next year, in 1877, the United States government tried to move the Nez Percé (NEZ PURS) tribe from their Oregon lands. Under Chief Joseph, the Indians headed towards Canada. The Nez Percé men, women, and children were outnumbered. But for a long time they held off the soldiers who were chasing them. Finally, Chief Joseph had to give up. He made a famous speech of surrender. "The little children are freezing to death," he said. "My people . . . have no blankets, no food . . . My heart is sick and sad. From where the sun now stands I will fight no more forever." This marked the end of big Indian fighting in Montana. Many of Montana's Indians were put on reservations.

Meanwhile, people learned that gold wasn't the only mineral in Montana. In 1881 Marcus Daly was looking for silver at Butte (BYOOT) Hill. He found copper. At first he was disappointed. But it turned out to be a very rich vein of copper. Marcus Daly later started a huge mining company—the Anaconda (an • ah • KON • dah) Company. Butte is still a great copper-mining center.

While some people were busy mining, others became ranchers. Cattle ranches were started. Cowboys watched

Berkeley Pit near Butte

the cattle. They branded them, so that people could tell which ranch owned the cattle. They rounded up the cattle. The building of railroads in the 1880s helped the cattle ranchers. The cattle were shipped by train to markets in the east. They were made into meat.

Starting in 1884, people wanted to make Montana a state. It took a few years before that happened. On November 8, 1889, Montana became our 41st state. Helena was its capital.

In the early 1900s, people discovered another treasure in eastern Montana. The land was good for growing

Cattle graze on Montana's grasslands while cowboys stand guard.

Wheat combine

wheat. Under the Enlarged Homestead Act of 1909, the land could be had for free! Like gold, free land brought people to Montana. Some put all their belongings in train boxcars. They went to Montana and set up wheat farms.

There were problems for the ranchers and the farmers. Freezing winters killed cattle. Summers without rain killed farm crops. Ranchers learned better ways to feed and care for their cattle in the winter. Farmers were helped by the building of dams. Dams store water. In times of no rain, the water is sent to farms. Bringing water to dry areas is called *irrigation* (ear • ih • GAY • shun).

A Montana woman made history in the early 1900s. Her name was Jeannette Rankin. When Jeannette was a girl, in 1890, most women were not allowed to vote. She worked to change that. In 1916 Jeannette Rankin was the first woman elected to the United States House of Representatives. Jeannette Rankin hated war. She was against the United States fighting in World War I and World War II. When she was 87 years old, she led a march against the Vietnam War. Jeannette Rankin died in 1973 at the age of 93.

In the 1950s one more treasure came from Montana ground. This was oil—called "black gold." Oil is needed to run cars and machinery. By the 1980s coal became a very important product.

Jeannette Rankin greets Vel Phillips at a protest march in Washington, D.C. The marchers called for an end to war and social injustice, causes Jeannette Rankin fought for all of her life.

Above: Conoco Refinery
Left: Workers dig for coal

Today, Montana is a leading state for producing oil, copper, coal, gold, and silver. It is a leading wheat-growing state. Montana is also a big state for raising beef cattle. Montana's mountains, forests, and old "ghost towns" make it one of the most interesting states to visit.

You have learned about some of Montana's history. Now it is time for a trip—in words and pictures—through the Treasure State.

On a map, Montana looks like a rectangle chipped away on one side. Canada is to the north of Montana. North and South Dakota are neighbor states to the east. Wyoming and part of Idaho are to the south. Idaho is the state to the west. Montana is a very large state. Only three states in the United States are bigger.

Pretend you're in an airplane high above Montana. In the eastern part of the state you will see some hills, but much of the land is flat. This land is part of the Great Plains. The mountains you see in the west are the Rocky Mountains.

Your airplane is landing in a city in Montana. This is Billings. It lies on the Yellowstone River. Billings was founded in 1882, when a railroad went through. Billings was named for the railroad president, Frederick Billings. Today, Billings is Montana's biggest city.

Billings, the state's biggest city

Ranchers raise cattle in the Billings area. The cattle
are turned into meat in Billings. Farmers grow sugar
beets and other crops nearby. The sugar beets are made
into sugar in Billings. Other foods are packed in Billings.
Oil is refined in the city.

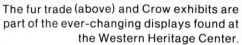

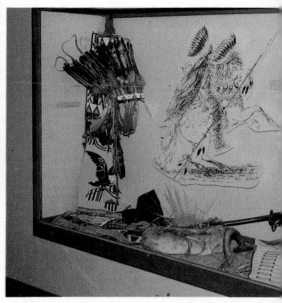

The fur trade (above) and Crow exhibits are part of the ever-changing displays found at the Western Heritage Center.

Visit the Western Heritage Center in Billings. There you can learn about Crow Indians, fur trappers, and homesteaders. The Yellowstone Art Center is fun, too. You can see art works there. You wouldn't want to have been there years ago, though. The building used to be a jail!

Billings is Montana's biggest city. But compared to the biggest cities in the United States, Billings is small. Its roughly 75,000 people could fit into a football stadium. Montana as a whole has fewer people than all but a few states. Montanans don't mind. Few people in a big state means that almost everyone has lots of room!

Go to Pictograph (PICK • toh • graph) Cave State Monument, near Billings. Indians made the pictures on the cave walls a long time ago. Pompey's Pillar is also near Billings. It is a 200-foot tall rock. You remember Sacagawea, who guided Lewis and Clark. She had a baby son, called Pompey, with her. Clark named Pompey's Pillar after the baby. Clark climbed part way up this rock on July 25, 1806. He carved his name and the date on it to prove he was there.

Left: Pompey's Pillar
Below: Indian markings at the
Medicine Man site

Traveling through eastern Montana, you can go long distances without seeing a town. You will see lots of ranches, farms, and wheat fields, though.

Wheat is used to make bread, breakfast cereals, and many other foods. Montana is a leading wheat-growing state. Machines do much of the work on the wheat farms. Machines called *drills* plant the wheat. Machines called *combines* are used to harvest it.

Wheat is the main crop, but not the only one. Hay, barley, sugar beets, cherries, and potatoes are other Montana crops. Sheep and hogs also are raised on farms.

In many areas, you will see fields sprinkled with water. The water is sent from rivers to farms. Without this irrigation water, parts of Montana would be like a desert in dry years.

Sheep

Have you noticed all those cattle in eastern Montana? The state has about 2.6 million cattle. That means there's more than three times as many cattle as people in Montana. Some of the cattle give milk. Most are used to make beef.

Raising beef cattle is a science as well as a business. Ranchers feed the cattle special diets so that they will produce good beef. They work to keep the cattle healthy. Cowboys still tend the cattle. Some cowboys work on horseback. But many now ride in trucks as they watch the cattle.

A rodeo rider at work

The cowboys know how to have fun, too. Many rodeos are held in Montana. At rodeos, cowboys see who can stay on bucking broncos the longest. They see who can rope cattle the fastest. The Midland Empire Fair and Rodeo in Billings is just one of Montana's many rodeos.

Southwest of Billings you will come to Yellowstone National Park. You can get there on a beautiful highway called Beartooth Highway. Most of Yellowstone National Park lies across the border in Wyoming. But part of it is in Montana.

North of Yellowstone National Park you will come to the city of Bozeman. It was named for John Bozeman, who blazed the famed Bozeman Trail during Montana's gold-rush days. Bozeman is in a big cattle-raising area. Milk and beef are two Bozeman products.

Montana State University is in Bozeman. Students there study farming. They also study history, science, and many other subjects.

Head to Butte, in southwestern Montana. Mining has been important to Butte for a long time. Gold brought the first settlers here in 1864. Later, silver and copper were found here. Today, a large amount of our country's copper is mined in Butte. There are old mine tunnels that go almost a mile deep right under the city!

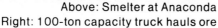
Above: Smelter at Anaconda
Right: 100-ton capacity truck hauls ore

Visit the World Museum of Mining in Butte. There you can learn how mining was done long ago as well as how it's done today. The Montana College of Mineral Science and Technology is in Butte. There students study to get jobs in the mining and oil industries.

Anaconda is very near Butte. You can't just dig up copper ore and use it to make pennies and wire. The copper has to be treated before it can be used to make things. Anaconda is one of the world's leading cities for processing copper.

State capitol
at Helena

Helena is northeast of Anaconda. When miners found gold here in 1864, the new town was called "Last Chance Gulch." The name was soon changed to Helena. Today, Helena is the capital of Montana.

Do you see that big building with the copper dome? That is the state capitol building. Lawmakers from all over Montana meet there. In recent years, they have worked on laws to protect the environment. They have worked to protect the state's wildlife. They have worked on many laws to help farmers and ranchers.

The Montana Historical Society is also in Helena. There you can learn about the history of the Treasure State.

Great Falls is about 90 miles northeast of Helena. Great Falls is the second largest city in Montana. Lewis and Clark were here in 1805. While exploring, Lewis was chased by a grizzly bear. The town was founded in the 1880s. It was named Great Falls because it lies at the big waterfalls of the Missouri River.

Metals and oil are refined in Great Falls. Meat is packed in the city. Flour is made there.

You'll enjoy the Charles M. Russell Original Studio and Museum in Great Falls. Russell was an artist who did pictures of the American West. You'll read more about him later.

Garnet is a ghost town.

There are some towns in western Montana that have few or no people. The buildings still stand. But the people left when they gave up looking for gold. These empty towns are called "ghost towns." You'll enjoy roaming through Elkhorn, Bearmouth, and other Montana ghost towns. Virginia City, in southwest Montana, isn't quite a ghost town because it has over 100 people. It has been rebuilt to look like it did in 1865, when it was a big gold-mining town.

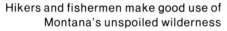
Hikers and fishermen make good use of
Montana's unspoiled wilderness

You've seen that this big state has many big things. It has big mines. It has big farms and ranches. On the wide plains in the east, even the sky looks big. In western Montana you see some very big mountains. These are the Rocky Mountains.

Take a trip through the Rockies. Some of the mountains are so high that they have never been climbed. Some have snow on their tops year-round. In the winter, many people ski in the Rockies. In warm weather, many camp and hike.

St. Mary Lake, Glacier National Park

Glacier National Park is in the Rocky Mountains of northwest Montana. You remember that, long ago, glaciers covered much of Montana. Would you like to see some glaciers? Over 50 of them remain in Glacier National Park.

You will see forests in the mountains—and in other regions of Montana. About a quarter of the state is forested. Douglas firs, pines, and spruces are some of the trees you'll find. Some trees are cut down. They are made into paper and wood products. But in some forests, woodcutting is not allowed. Such forests will always be there for people to enjoy.

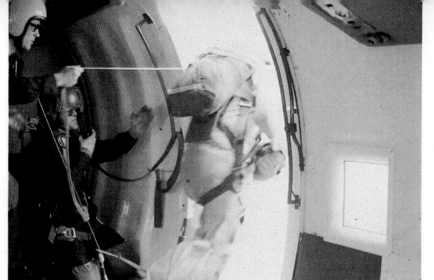

A smoke jumper
bails out

Fire is a big enemy of Montana's forests. There are lookout towers in Montana. From the towers, rangers watch for fires. The U.S. Forest Service has a headquarters at Missoula, in western Montana. Some fire fighters trained at Missoula are called *smoke jumpers*. They jump out of planes and parachute down to fight forest fires.

People aren't the only ones who enjoy Montana's forests and mountains. A great amount of wildlife is another of the state's treasures. In the mountains you may run across some bears. There are black bears and grizzly bears in the state. Grizzlies can weigh over 800 pounds. You can see beavers building their dams on mountain streams. Mountain goats, mountain sheep, and

Wildlife abounds in Montana. The mountain goat (top left), elk (top right), bighorn sheep (left), and the bull moose (above) roam freely in the mountains.

mountain lions enjoy the high places. Moose, elk, deer, and porcupines can also be found in the mountains. There are even a few wolves left.

The plains also have interesting animals. Pronghorn antelopes like to run along the level land. They can run 60 miles per hour. Coyotes live on the plains. Farmers dislike them, because they kill sheep. Prairie dogs can also be found in the flat areas. They aren't dogs. They are members of the squirrel family.

The western meadow lark (above) is the state bird of Montana. The bald eagle (right) is the symbol of the United States of America.

There are also many kinds of birds in Montana. You'll see ducks, geese, swans, and grouse. The bald eagle—our nation's symbol—can be seen in Montana. Some of the birds fly south for the winter. Montana is so far north that its winters are VERY cold. The state's record low temperature is −70°. That's the coldest it's ever been in the United States—except for Alaska.

Montana has another weather record. In 1916, at Browning, the temperature changed 100° in one day. It went from 44° to −56°. That's the biggest change for a one-day period ever recorded in our country.

Finish your Montana trip by visiting the Blackfeet Indian reservation in northwest Montana. There are about 45,000 Indians from at least 10 major tribes in Montana today. The Blackfeet, Crow, Assiniboine, and Sioux are four of the main tribes. Roughly half the Indians live on the state's seven reservations. The other half live in many places throughout Montana.

Indians work at almost every kind of job. Some are teachers, doctors, lawyers, and miners. Some are fire fighters. Some tribes own their own businesses. The Blackfeet have their own pencil factory. The Assiniboine and Sioux have made military items for the United States government.

The Indian people keep their old ways alive. Children are taught English as well as the tribal language. They are taught the stories, dances, and games of their people. Children also learn beadwork and how to make Indian costumes.

Many old ceremonies are held. Indians have naming ceremonies. At these events, an Indian name is given to a child or an adult. Afterwards, there is often a giveaway. The family of the person being named gives gifts to the guests.

Places can't tell the whole story of Montana. Many interesting people have lived in the Treasure State.

Granville Stuart (1834-1918) was born in what is now West Virginia. As a young man, he moved to Montana. The story of Stuart's life is much like the history of Montana. He traded with the Indians and married an Indian woman. He was one of the first to find gold in Montana. He also raised cattle. Rustlers sometimes stole the ranchers' cattle. Granville Stuart formed a vigilante group. They caught and hanged the rustlers. Throughout his life, Stuart taught himself by reading. He once rode 150 miles (and spent about half his money) to get some books. Granville Stuart also wrote his own books on the history of Montana.

This is the real thing
painted the winter of 1886
at the OH ranch
C M Russell

This picture is Char.
Russell's reply to
inquiry as to the
condition of
in 1886. L E Kaufman

Reproduction of the drawing and note made by Charles M. Russell in 1886

Charles M. Russell (1864-1926) was born in St. Louis,
Missouri. He, too, moved to Montana as a young man.
Russell lived as a hunter for a while. Later, he worked as
a cowboy. Russell liked to draw pictures of cowboys,
Indians, and animals. During the very cold winter of
1886-1887, Russell painted a famous picture. It showed a
dying cow about to fall into the snow as wolves stood
close by. Better than words could, this picture showed
what winter storms had done to the cattle business.
Charles Russell drew many Western pictures.

Gary Cooper (1901-1961) was born in Helena. He tended cattle on his family's ranch. Cooper became a famous movie star. *High Noon, The Westerner, Sergeant York,* and *The Hanging Tree* are just four of his films.

Chet Huntley (1911-1974) was born in Cardwell, Montana. As a boy, he lived on a ranch. Huntley was very good at giving speeches in school. He got a job as a radio announcer. Later Chet Huntley became a famous T.V. newscaster.

Mike Mansfield was born in New York City in 1903. But he grew up in Montana. He worked as a miner in Montana copper mines. Later, Mansfield became a lawmaker. Like Jeannette Rankin, he served in the United States House of Representatives. Then he served in the United States Senate. Mansfield was the "majority leader" of the Senate for 16 years. No other person has ever held that job so long.

Home to Blackfeet Indians ... miners ... farmers ...
ranchers ... and grizzly bears.

Birthplace of Jeannette Rankin and Gary Cooper.

A beautiful land of mountains ... rivers ... and broad
plains.

A top wheat-growing and copper-mining state.

This is beautiful Montana—the Treasure State!

Grant-Kohrs Ranch

Facts About MONTANA

Area—147,138 square miles (our 4th biggest state)

Greatest Distance North to South—318 miles

Greatest Distance East to West—550 miles

Borders—The country of Canada to the north; the states of North Dakota and South Dakota to the east; Wyoming and part of Idaho to the south; Idaho to the west

Highest Point—12,799 feet above sea level (Granite Peak)

Lowest Point—1,800 feet above sea level (the Kootenai River)

Hottest Recorded Temperature—117° (at Glendive, on July 20, 1893, and also at Medicine Lake, on July 5, 1937)

Coldest Recorded Temperature—Minus 70° (at Rogers Pass, on January 20, 1954)

Statehood—Our 41st state, on November 8, 1889

Origin of Name—The word *Montana* comes from the Spanish word *montaña*, which means *mountain*

Capital—Helena

Previous Capitals—Bannack and Virginia City

Counties— 56

U.S. Senators—2

U.S. Representatives—2

State Senators—50

State Representatives—100

State Song—"Montana" by Charles C. Cohen and Joseph E. Howard

State Motto— *Oro y Plata* (Spanish meaning "Gold and Silver")

Main Nickname—The Treasure State

Some Other Nicknames—Big Sky Country, the Land of the Shining Mountains, the Bonanza State, the Stubtoe State

State Seal— ^ ·

State Fl·

S

State Stones

Some Rivers—Missouri, Yellowstone, Marias, Milk, Musselshell, Clark Fork,
   Bitterroot, Flathead, Kootenai, Judith
Biggest Natural Lake—Flathead Lake
Biggest Man-made Lake—Fort Peck Lake
Indian Reservations—7
National Parklands—Glacier National Park
                    Fort Benton
                    Grant-Kohrs Ranch National Historic Site
                    Big Hole National Battlefield
                    Bighorn Canyon National Recreation Area
                    Custer Battlefield National Monument
                    Yellowstone National Park
National Forests—11
Montana State Parks, Monuments, and Recreation Areas—87
Wildlife—Black bears, grizzly bears, deer, elk, moose, mountain goats, mountain
   sheep, mountain lions, bobcats, wolverines, wolves, pronghorn antelopes,
   coyotes, prairie dogs, gophers, rabbits, pack rats, ducks, geese, swans, grouse,
   pheasants, bald eagles, many other kinds of birds, rattlesnakes
Fishing—Trout, grayling, bass, whitefish
Farm Products—Beef cattle, milk, sheep, hogs, eggs, wheat, oats, barley, rye,
   sugar beets, potatoes, cherries, corn
Mining—Oil, copper, coal, natural gas, silver, gold, vermiculite, limestone
Manufacturing—Lumber, wood products, packed meat, flour, sugar, many other
   packaged food products, chemicals, metal products, petroleum products, coal
   products
Population—761,000 (1977 estimate; the 43rd most populous state)
Major Cities— Billings   73,500   (1979 estimate)
               Great Falls   60,200   (1979 estimate)
               Missoula   29,600   (1979 estimate)
               Helena   28,700   (1979 estimate)
               Butte   22,608   (1976 estimate)
               Bozeman   19,200   (1979 estimate)

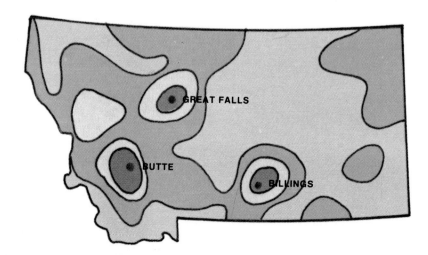

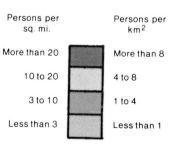

Persons per sq. mi.		Persons per km²
More than 20		More than 8
10 to 20		4 to 8
3 to 10		1 to 4
Less than 3		Less than 1

Montana History

There were people in Montana at least 10,000 years ago.

1740s—French fur trappers may have entered Montana

1803—Most of Montana becomes a United States territory by the Louisiana Purchase

1805—American explorers Lewis and Clark pass through Montana on their way to the Pacific Ocean. Sacagawea (also spelled Sacajawea) was their guide

1806—Lewis and Clark pass through Montana on their way back east

1807—Manuel Lisa builds the first fur-trading post in Montana

1841—Father Pierre Jean De Smet founds St. Mary's Mission in Montana; he soon leads the planting of the first crops in Montana

1846—All of Montana now belongs to the United States; this same year Montana's first permanent settlement, Fort Lewis (later called Fort Benton) is founded

1862—Big gold find at Grasshopper Creek; the town of Bannack is founded there

1863—Gold rush to Alder Gulch, where Virginia City is founded; John Bozeman starts building the Bozeman Trail to the gold fields

1864—Montana Territory is created; there is a gold rush to Last Chance Gulch, where Helena is built

1875—Helena becomes the capital of the Montana Territory

1876—Sioux and Cheyenne Indians wipe out Custer and his men in the Battle of the Little Bighorn

1877—After fighting bravely, Chief Joseph and the Nez Percé are forced to surrender to the U.S. Army in Montana

1880—Railroad enters Montana; Jeannette Rankin is born near Missoula

1883—State is crossed by a railroad

1889—On November 8, Montana becomes our 41st state

1895—The University of Montana opens in Missoula

1900—Population of the Treasure State is 243,329

1910—Glacier National Park is established

1910-1917—Many homesteaders go to eastern Montana to farm

1916—Jeannette Rankin becomes the first woman elected to the U.S. House of Representatives

1930—Population has zoomed to 537,606

1935—Helena is jolted by earthquakes

1940—Fort Peck Dam is completed; it helps provide irrigation water

1951—Oil boom in eastern Montana begins

1959—Earthquake hits state and creates Quake Lake

1964—Terrible flood causes deaths and damage to property

1966—Yellowtail Dam is finished

1973—Present state constitution goes into effect; in this same year Jeannette Rankin dies

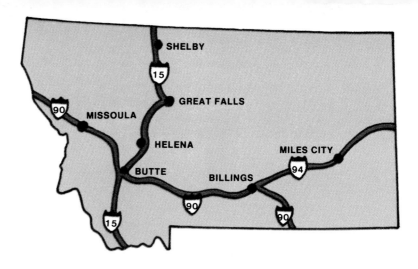

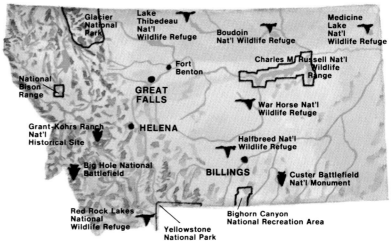

INDEX

47

INDEX, Cont'd

About the Author:

Dennis Fradin attended Northwestern University on a creative writing scholarship and graduated in 1967. While still at Northwestern, he published his first stories in *Ingenue* magazine and also won a prize in *Seventeen's* short story competition. A prolific writer, Dennis Fradin has been regularly publishing stories in such diverse places as *The Saturday Evening Post, Scholastic, National Humane Review, Midwest,* and *The Teaching Paper.* He has also scripted several educational films. Since 1970 he has taught second grade reading in a Chicago school—a rewarding job, which, the author says, "provides a captive audience on whom I test my children's stories." Married and the father of three children, Dennis Fradin spends his free time with his family or playing a myriad of sports and games with his childhood chums.

About the Artists:

Len Meents studied painting and drawing at Southern Illinois University and after graduation in 1969 he moved to Chicago. Mr. Meents works full time as a painter and illustrator. He and his wife and child currently make their home in LaGrange, Illinois.

Richard Wahl, graduate of the Art Center College of Design in Los Angeles, has illustrated a number of magazine articles and booklets. He is a skilled artist and photographer who advocates realistic interpretations of his subjects. He lives with his wife and two sons in Libertyville, Illinois.